Print Handwriting Workbook for Teens

Practice Workbook with Amazing Historical Facts that Build Knowledge in a Young Teenager

Legal & Disclaimer

The information contained in this book and its contents are not designed to replace or take the place of any form of medical or professional advice. The information provided by this book is not meant to replace the need for independent medical, financial, legal or other professional advice or services, as may be required.

The content and information contained in this book have been compiled from sources deemed reliable and are accurate to the best of the Author's knowledge and belief. The Author cannot, however, guarantee its accuracy and validity and cannot be held liable for any errors and/or omissions. When needed, further changes will be periodically made to this book. Where appropriate and/or necessary, you agree and are obligated to consult a professional before using any information in this book.

Upon using the contents and information contained in this book, you agree to hold the Author harmless from and against any damages, costs, and expenses, including any legal fees potentially resulting from the application of any of the information provided by this book. This disclaimer applies to any loss, damages or injury caused by the use and application, whether directly or indirectly, of any advice or information presented, whether for breach of contract, tort, negligence, personal injury, criminal intent, or under any other cause of action.

You agree to accept all risks of using the information presented in this book.

Disclaimer Note:
While we try to provide the most accurate information possible.
Please note that each scientific field is subjected to constant discoveries.
That's why the facts included in this book
might be proven wrong or might be updated in the years to come.
However, our goal here is to spark your curiosity and
offer an interesting and enjoyable handwriting experience.

Introduction to Print Handwriting

The goal of this workbook is to help you develop or improve your print handwriting skills. It is designed for beginners and intermediates since it mostly focuses on the writing in print style of entire words and sentences.

This book does, however, contain a short practice section for each letter. This overview includes recommendations on how each letter should be written. The rest of the workbook contains fun and intriguing historical facts about ancient civilizations like:

- *Ancient Greece*
- *Ancient Persia*
- *Ancient Rome*
- *Ancient Egypt*
- *Ancient China*

Each exercise is composed of two sections. The first section contains specific words extracted from the sentence and written with a traceable print font. The second section contains a worksheet designed for the sentence to be rewritten in its entirety.

While I highly endorse cursive handwriting because of its scientifically proven benefits. Print handwriting doesn't go without its merits. It can help you develop a neat and legible writing style. It's therefore important, in my opinion, to master both cursive and print handwriting styles. This workbook focuses on the latter.

The historical facts inside this book can offer you meaningful insight into our cultures of origin as well as cultures which might be less familiar to you. All that while also improving your handwriting skills. The acquired knowledge can spark interesting conversations in your daily life with both friends and family.

Print uppercase letters

Print lowercase letters

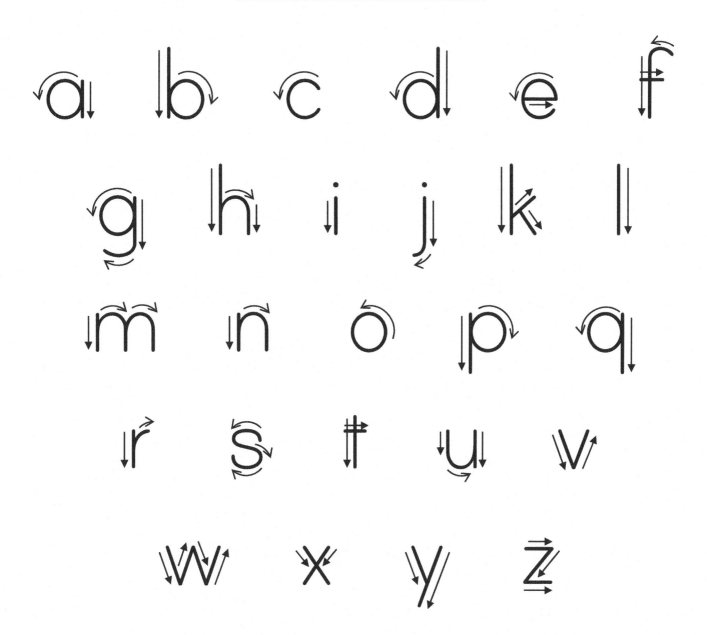

Print letter practice

A

a

B

b

C

c

D

d

E

E

F

f

O

Q

H

h

I

j

J

O

P

p

O

Q

R

r

S

s

T

Historical Fact No.1 – Ancient Greece

The first Ancient Greek civilizations were formed approximately 4000 years ago by the Myceneans of Crete.

Ancient   Ancient Ancient Ancient

Ancient Ancient Ancient

Greek   Greek

formed

years

Copy the entire previous quote below while using your best handwriting.

Historical Fact No.2 – Ancient Greece

The ancient Greeks were superstitious and did not eat beans, as they believed these contained the souls of the dead.

beans

believed

contained

souls

Copy the entire previous quote below while using your best handwriting.

Historical Fact No.3 – Ancient Greece

Until they turned 30 and were allowed to leave the military service, Spartan soldiers were not permitted to live with their families.

turned

allowed

military

Spartan

Copy the entire previous quote below while using your best handwriting.

Historical Fact No.4 – Ancient Greece

The ancient Olympic Games were considered a religious event and were held to honor Zeus. Zeus was thought to be the father of the Greek gods and goddesses.

Olympic

considered

religious

held

Copy the entire previous quote below while using your best handwriting.

Historical Fact No.5 — Ancient Greece

One of the most significant battles in human history was the Battle of Salamis. Taking place in 480 BC, it was fought between an alliance of Greek city-states and the Persian Empire, which was then ruled by King Xerxes. It is believed that if the Persians had won, it would have changed Western civilization as we know it today.

battles

history

Salamis

alliance

Copy the entire previous quote below while using your best handwriting.

Historical Fact No.6 – Ancient Greece

Alexander the Great became king in the year 336 BC following his father's death. During his lifetime, he conquered most of the world known to the ancient Greeks.

king

following

lifetime

world

Copy the entire previous quote below while using your best handwriting.

After the battle of Corinth in 146 BC, the Romans took control over the Greek peninsula.

battle

Corinth

Romans

control

Copy the entire previous quote below while using your best handwriting.

Historical Fact No.8 - Ancient Persia

The Persian Empire began on the Iranian plateau as a collection of semi-nomadic tribes who raised sheep, goats and cattle.

Persian

Empire

began

plateau

Copy the entire previous quote below while using your best handwriting.

Historical Fact No.9 – Ancient Persia

The founder of the Persian Empire was Cyrus the Great. It was also known as the Achaemenid Empire and was founded in the year 550 BC.

founder

Cyrus

founded

year

Copy the entire previous quote below while using your best handwriting.

Historical Fact No.10 – Ancient Persia

While under the rule of Cyrus the Great, the Persians allowed the people they conquered to continue their lives and cultures. This meant that as long as they obeyed the Persian rules and paid taxes, they could keep their traditions and religions.

While

conquered

obeyed

traditions

Copy the entire previous quote below while using your best handwriting.

Historical Fact No.11 – Ancient Persia

Since the Persian Empire was so large, each area had a designated ruler called a satrap (similar to a modern-day governor) in order to maintain control.

Since

large

called

satrap

Copy the entire previous quote below while using your best handwriting.

The capital of the Achaemenid Empire (Persian Empire) was a city called Persepolis.

capital

city

called

Persepolis

Copy the entire previous quote below while using your best handwriting.

Historical Fact No.13 – Ancient Persia

Artaxerxes II was the longest reigning Persian king. He ruled for 45 years and for this duration, the Persian Empire enjoyed a time of peace and prosperity.

longest

reigning

king

peace

Copy the entire previous quote below while using your best handwriting.

The Persians considered lying to be one of the most disgraceful acts someone could commit.

acts

someone

could

commit

Copy the entire previous quote below while using your best handwriting.

Historical Fact No.15 – Ancient Persia

"The Immortals" were an elite infantry of the Persian Empire. Each solider was heavily armed and this force acted as both an imperial guard and a standing army.

elite

infantry

heavily

armed

Copy the entire previous quote below while using your best handwriting.

Historical Fact No.16 – Ancient Persia

The Persian Empire started a period of decline in 480 BC following a failed invasion of Greece by King Xerxes.

failed

invasion

King

Xerxes

Copy the entire previous quote below while using your best handwriting.

In the year 330 BC, the Persian Empire fell after the successful invasion of Alexander the Great.

year

fell

after

invasion

Copy the entire previous quote below while using your best handwriting.

The Roman Civilization began on the Italian Peninsula during the 8th century BC.

began

Italian

during

century

Copy the entire previous quote below while using your best handwriting.

Historical Fact No.19 – Ancient Rome

The founder of the Roman civilization was Romulus.
Legend has it that Romulus and his twin brother, Remus,
were abandoned as babies and raised by a female wolf.
Romulus then became the first ruler of Rome after
fighting and defeating his brother.

founder

legend

twin

brother

Copy the entire previous quote below while using your best handwriting.

Augustus Caesar founded the Roman Empire in the year 27 BC and was granted the title of Emperor.

Augustus

Caesar

title

Emperor

Copy the entire previous quote below while using your best handwriting.

Historical Fact No.21 – Ancient Rome

The Roman Empire included, at the height of its power, Italy, all the lands surrounding the Mediterranean Sea, and a large part of Europe.

included

height

power

Italy

Copy the entire previous quote below while using your best handwriting.

The Roman Empire is famous for its strong military. The Roman army could walk up to 40 km in a single day.

famous

strong

military

army

Copy the entire previous quote below while using your best handwriting.

Historical Fact No.23 – Ancient Rome

Although it's extremely well-known in today's society, the Roman Empire was only the 28th largest Empire in the world's history and contained just 12% of the world's population at that time.

society

largest

history

time

Copy the entire previous quote below while using your best handwriting.

Historical Fact No.24 – Ancient Rome

In addition to being excellent fighters, the Romans were also great engineers and architects. Their inventions had a great influence on the world as we know it today.

addition

fighters

world

today

Copy the entire previous quote below while using your best handwriting.

Historical Fact No.25 - Ancient Rome

The Romans were extremely fond of theatre. In order to perform mock sea battles, they used to flood the entire Colosseum.

fond

theatre

perform

mock

Copy the entire previous quote below while using your best handwriting.

Historical Fact No.26 – Ancient Rome

Romans used to enjoy eating with their hands while lying on a couch. They would rarely use a spoon, but never a knife and fork.

eating

hands

lying

couch

Copy the entire previous quote below while using your best handwriting.

The Roman Emperor, Gaius Caligula, made his horse a senator.

Gaius

Caligula

horse

senator

Copy the entire previous quote below while using your best handwriting.

Historical Fact No.28 – Ancient Rome

During the reign of Trajan, between 98 - 117 AD, the Roman Empire reached its greatest geographical extent. During that period, it covered approximately 5 million square km.

Trajan

reached

greatest

extent

Copy the entire previous quote below while using your best handwriting.

Historical Fact No.29 – Ancient Egypt

The mummification process was performed in Ancient Egypt because they believed that in order for the dead to be reborn in the afterlife, the body needed to be preserved.

believed

order

reborn

afterlife

Copy the entire previous quote below while using your best handwriting.

More than 1000 gods and goddesses were worshipped in Ancient Egypt.

More

than

gods

Egypt

Copy the entire previous quote below while using your best handwriting.

Historical Fact No.31 – Ancient Egypt

Animals were also mummified in Ancient Egypt. They were viewed not only as pets, but also as incarnations of gods.

Animals

viewed

pets

gods

Copy the entire previous quote below while using your best handwriting.

Tutankhamun was the youngest Pharaoh to rule in Ancient Egypt.

youngest

Pharaoh

rule

Egypt

Copy the entire previous quote below while using your best handwriting.

The Eye of Horus was an Egyptian symbol which represented royal power, protection, and good health.

Eye

Horus

symbol

health

Copy the entire previous quote below while using your best handwriting.

Historical Fact No.34 – Ancient Egypt

Egyptian rulers were always depicted as athletic and slim; however, it is believed that most of them were obese and lived an unhealthy lifestyle.

rulers

always

depicted

slim

Copy the entire previous quote below while using your best handwriting.

The Ancient Egyptian civilization lasted more than 3000 years, from 3150 BC to 30 BC.

lasted

more

than

from

Copy the entire previous quote below while using your best handwriting.

Historical Fact No.36 – Ancient Egypt

The statue of the Sphinx was constructed more than 4500 years ago. It was viewed as a guardian to the pyramid of Khafre at Giza.

statue

Sphinx

viewed

guardian

Copy the entire previous quote below while using your best handwriting.

Historical Fact No.37 – Ancient China

The first Chinese emperor was called Shi Huangdi. He united and subjugated the Warring States in 221 BC and formed China.

first

Chinese

emperor

united

Copy the entire previous quote below while using your best handwriting.

Historical Fact No.38 – Ancient China

Legend says that the Chinese Goddess, Nu Gua, decided to create humanity because she did not want the Yellow River to remain quiet and alone.

Legend

humanity

remain

quiet

Copy the entire previous quote below while using your best handwriting.

Historical Fact No.39 – Ancient China

At first, the Great Wall of China was built in smaller segments by individual Chinese states. It was only later on that these segments were joined together to become a single wall.

Great

Wall

built

smaller

Copy the entire previous quote below while using your best handwriting.

Historical Fact No.40 – Ancient China

The purpose of the Great Wall of China was to protect the Chinese Empire from the Mongolians and other invaders.

purpose

protect

from

invaders

Copy the entire previous quote below while using your best handwriting.

Historical Fact No.41 – Ancient China

The ancient Chinese considered Yu the Great to be one of their greatest rulers ever. He was a brilliant engineer who introduced flood control and established the Xia Dynasty.

greatest

rulers

brilliant

engineer

Copy the entire previous quote below while using your best handwriting.

Chinese Emperors thought of the dragon as a symbol of strength, power and good fortune.

thought

dragon

symbol

strength

Copy the entire previous quote below while using your best handwriting.

Ancient Chinese writers used bamboo strips to write on before paper was invented.

writers

used

bamboo

strips

Copy the entire previous quote below while using your best handwriting.

Historical Fact No.44 – Ancient China

In ancient China, doctors would receive payment only if the patient was cured. If, however, the patient started to feel worse, the doctor would have to pay the patient.

doctors

receive

payment

cured

Copy the entire previous quote below while using your best handwriting.

Historical Fact No.45 – Ancient China

Visitors to the Royal Court were required to show respect to their ruler by kneeling and tapping their forehead on the ground nine times.

Visitors

Court

show

respect

Copy the entire previous quote below while using your best handwriting.

Made in the USA
Monee, IL
08 September 2020